MIKHAIL GORBACHEV

by Anna Sproule

Picture Credits

Brian Harris — 55; The Hulton Photographic Library — 7; Keston College Photo Archive — 33; Magnum Photos Ltd. — Eric Lessing 6: Ian Berry 18, 25: Henri Cartier-Bresson 27: Burt Glinn 28, 29: Franco Zecchin 32, 56 (above): Peter Marlow 37: Abbas 58; Novosti 36; The Society for Cultural Relations with the USSR — 16 (below), 20, 34, 35, 42, 43, 46; Frank Spooner Pictures — V. Shone/Gamma 4: Chip Hires/Gamma 8 (above), 9 (above): Patrick Peal/Gamma 8 (below): G. Merrilon/Gamma 9 (below): Felici/Gamma 11: A.P.N./Gamma 12: Daniel Simon/Gamma 13, 30: Novosti/Gamma 22, 40, 41, 48: Blanche/ Gamma 41 (above): Tass/Gamma 41 (below): Merrilon/Piel/Gamma 51: Bouvet/Gamma 53 (above): Bouvet/Merrilon/Gamma 53 (below): Zola/Gamma 56 (below): Merrilon/Gamma 57 (above): Bassinac/Gamma 57 (below), 60.

North American edition first published in 1991 by
Gareth Stevens Children's Books
1555 North RiverCenter Drive, Suite 201
Milwaukee, Wisconsin 53212, USA

First published in the United Kingdom in 1991 by Exley Publications with an original text by Anna Sproule. Additional end matter copyright © 1991 by Gareth Stevens, Inc.
All rights reserved. No part of this book may be reproduced or used in any form or by any means without permission in writing from Gareth Stevens, Inc.

Library of Congress Cataloging-in-Publication Data

Sproule, Anna.
    Mikhail Gorbachev / by Anna Sproule.
        p. cm. — (People who have helped the world)
    Includes index.
    Summary: An account of Mr. Gorbachev's role in the Soviet Union at the present time, as events unfold which portend a much freer way of life for the Russian people.
    ISBN 0-8368-0401-5
    1. Gorbachev, Mikhail Sergeyevich, 1931-   —Juvenile literature. 2. Heads of state—Soviet Union—Biography—Juvenile literature. 3. Soviet Union—Politics and government—1917-   —Juvenile literature. [1. Gorbachev, Mikhail Sergeyevich, 1931-   . 2. Heads of state. 3. Soviet Union—Politics and government—1917-]
I. Title. II. Series.
DK290.3.G67S6   1990   [B]   [92]   90-10010
947.085'4'092—dc20

Series conceived and edited by Helen Exley
Series editor, U.S.: Rhoda Irene Sherwood
Editor, U.S.: Tom Barnett
Editorial assistant, U.S.: Diane Laska
Research editors, U.S.: Meredith Ackley and John D. Rateliff
Copy editor, U.S.: Scott Enk

Printed in Hungary

1 2 3 4 5 6 7 8 9 94 93 92 91

MIKHAIL GORBACHEV

Revolutionary for democracy

by Anna Sproule

Gareth Stevens Children's Books
MILWAUKEE

When the nightmares fade

It was a day when nightmares faded, and a day when dreams came true. In a cruise ship moored off the storm-battered coast of Malta, the leaders of the world's two most powerful countries had just pledged themselves to peace. As the wind howled outside, excited journalists crowded into the lounge of the ship *Maxim Gorky* to hear the news.

A few months earlier, what they heard would have been the story of the year — perhaps even of the decade. George Bush, president of the United States, and Mikhail Gorbachev, president of the Union of Soviet Socialist Republics, stood before them to announce the end of the cold war. This was a war for military supremacy in which almost no shots were fired. It had endured since the close of World War II.

The tension, the deadly rivalry, the whole cloud of fear and hatred that had grown up between the West and the world of the Communist East since World War II had disappeared. The Soviet Union, Mikhail Gorbachev declared, would never start a "hot war" against the United States.

"And I'm sure," Gorbachev said, "the president of the United States would never start a war against us." President Bush, when asked if the cold war was really over, replied with a jubilant thumbs up.

But this was the last month of 1989. And the end of the cold war was just one amazing headline among many. By the time the two world leaders made their announcement on December 3, the unbelievable had become almost commonplace.

The nightmares were fading all across Eastern Europe, from the Black Sea to the Baltic Sea. The impossible was impossible no longer. And the wildest, most fantastic, most incredible dreams were coming true every day.

Opposite: A day for smiling. George Bush and Mikhail Gorbachev, presidents of the United States and the Union of Soviet Socialist Republics, come together on the Soviet cruise ship Maxim Gorky *to declare the end of the cold war.*

5

No funeral for "Mr. Strach"

In Czechoslovakia, for instance, the dream that came true was a death — the death of a mythical monster that the Czechs called "Mr. Strach."

Families in central Europe announce deaths by putting up mourning posters with thick black borders. A poster of Mr. Strach appeared in Czechoslovakia's capital, Prague, in its famous Wenceslas Square. A statue of Saint Wenceslas, the patron saint of Czecho-slovakia, stared benignly over crowds of Czechs as they chuckled at what the poster said.

The deceased, it stated in mock-formal tones, had died on November 17, 1989, much mourned by the police. There would be no funeral.

Strach, in Czech, means "fear." "Mr. Strach" was the name the Czechs use to refer to the system of control that the government used to rule the country.

In Czechoslovakia, fear and oppression had been a big part of most people's lives. The Czechs who confronted it in mid-November were students. On the day Mr. Strach's death was announced, fifty thousand of them staged a peaceful protest against the all-powerful Communist government that had run the country since the end of World War II.

Where the protest ended, not far from Wenceslas Square, the students had created a barrier out of lit candles marking two lines on the road.

Surrounded by the soft glow of the flickering barriers, three thousand of these protesters sat on the ground, held their hands up in the air, and broke into a chant of "No violence!"

Like a massive, moving wall, the state riot police bore down on the students, shields and clubs in their hands. As they approached the protesters, the chanting students offered them red carnations and sweet-scented red roses.

In response, the riot police kicked over the flickering candles, attacked the protesters, and started to beat them with their clubs.

What the bells said

Earlier protests by the Czech people had been dealt with harshly by the Soviets. In 1968, reforms known as

After World War II, the countries of Eastern Europe fell under the Soviet Union's power. They became part of an enormous Communist empire that stretched from central Germany to the Bering Strait. The man in the picture is one of the hundreds of thousands of Hungarians who, in October 1956, rose in anti-Soviet revolt. Soviet tanks that rolled in crushed the revolution.

the "Prague Spring" were put into effect. These reforms relaxed many of the restrictions which had limited the freedom of the Czech people. The Soviet government felt that these reforms were a threat to their control of the government of Czechoslovakia.

So in August of that year, the Soviet government responded. They sent tanks and other military units into the capital city, Prague, to restore the much more restrictive rules and guidelines.

The Soviets wanted to eliminate the reforms, but they also wanted to send a message to the other countries that were controlled by the Soviet government. The message was that there would be a heavy price to pay for attempts to question Soviet authority on running the government. None of the countries were in a position to stand up against the military strength of the Soviet army.

Order was restored in Czechoslovakia, but the people who organized the reforms and the citizens who had enjoyed the increased freedom did not give up their desire for change.

Twelve years after the Hungarian Revolution, the Czech people also tried to free themselves from Soviet Communism. In 1968, they introduced sweeping reforms. People were allowed to say what they thought about the government. Even non-Communist groups were allowed to take part in politics. But this "Prague Spring" of reform ended on August 20, 1968, when Soviet troops like these moved in and took over.

But in November 1989, things turned out differently. The Soviet tanks did not come to back up the Czech military in dispersing the protesters. Realizing that the Czech government did not have the support of the Soviet army, the people increased their protests and fought back. This time they were able to achieve their dream of changing the system.

"Mr. Strach" was dead, and the rule of the Communist party was in its last days. Bells everywhere rang gleefully, marking the end of an era of fear and control. Huge crowds celebrated their newfound freedom.

The prison state

In East Germany, people were joking and laughing, too. The eastern part of Germany had turned to Communism after World War II. But now, in East Berlin, the people were wearing T-shirts that read

At the Berlin Wall. Between 1961, when the wall was built, and 1989, when it was opened, over one hundred East Germans died trying to escape to the West. Some lie buried at its foot (opposite, below). Above and left: Two faces of joy as the wall is breached: garlanded with flowers, a soldier smiles broadly, while a woman weeps. Armed with hammer and chisel, the young Berliner in the large picture (opposite, above) chips away at the wall.

"Last one out, turn out the light." "Out" meant "out of the country."

For over forty years, Communist-ruled East Germany had seemed like a prison to many of its people. Few people were allowed to move out of the country, unless they were too old to work. Crossing the well-guarded frontier that divided East Germany from the world of the West was an unthinkable act.

For twenty-eight years, the East Germans had regarded one part of that frontier with special hatred. Through their capital city ran an ugly concrete barrier, lined with watchtowers and manned by fourteen thousand armed guards. It was the infamous Berlin Wall. Built in 1961, the wall divided the German city of Berlin right down the middle. To Germans who were proud of their historic capital, the wall was an insult and a disgrace. This ugly monument to the divided

9

nation came to symbolize the tension and desire for escape that it contained.

By 1989, one hundred East Germans had died as they tried to cross this dreadful barrier to escape to the West. Some had drowned swimming one of Berlin's waterways. Some had broken their necks jumping from buildings that overlooked the border. But most had been shot by the guards who guarded the wall.

The wall opens

The nightmare went on and on. It looked as if it would continue into the twenty-first century. But suddenly everything changed. In Hungary, another Communist country, the government removed restrictions which had made it impossible to leave the country. East Germans who were vacationing in Hungary were able to leave and escape to the West through these borders. Defying their government, thousands streamed west through every gap they could find in the border.

The East German leaders raged and threatened, but in vain. The numbers of people escaping climbed daily. And then, in a desperate bid to placate their defiant country, the Communists did the unbelievable. On Thursday, November 9, 1989, they opened the Berlin Wall.

Cheering, laughing, and blasting car horns, East Berliners poured through the gaps as fast as the bull-dozers could make them. The younger people climbed the hated barrier and surveyed the hidden world of West Berlin in triumph. Some attacked the wall with hammers, chipping at the concrete. Others danced, sang, and threw flowers to the guards down below.

Older people, who could remember when the Berlin Wall was built, wept in dazed joy as they walked through the streets of West Berlin that they'd been kept out of for so long.

Young and old, they were all sure of one thing. No one would ever keep them shut in again.

"We do not conceal our attitude to the religious outlook as being non-materialistic and unscientific. But this is no reason for a disrespectful attitude to the spiritual-minded-ness of the believer."

Mikhail Gorbachev, addressing a special Communist party conference, June 1988

The pope and the president

As the winter of 1989 closed in, the unbelievable took place in Eastern Europe. Like the mythical Mr. Strach in Czechoslovakia, fear was totally eliminated, not just in Prague but in Romania, Hungary, and Yugoslavia, as well as in most of the other Communist countries in this region, known as the Eastern bloc countries. But that was not all. Impossible dreams came true in the West as well.

On December 1, a big, black car swept through Rome to Saint Peter's Square and the tiny state of the Vatican. In the car, with his wife, rode Mikhail Gorbachev, the president of a country that had declared the practice of religion to be illegal. In this country, the Soviet Union, many people had been persecuted for their religious beliefs. The president of this country was on his way to visit Pope John Paul II.

In the Vatican, the pope's residence, the leader of the world's Roman Catholics warmly welcomed the head of a country of 280 million people. It was the first time a pope had met the head of the Soviet Union since the Russian Revolution had brought the Communist state into being in 1917. By the time the two men parted, the Polish-born pope had received an invitation to Moscow. And the Soviet president had guaranteed freedom of worship for everyone in his huge country.

The pope meets the Soviet president and the president's wife.

11

Celebrating the might of Soviet Communism, 1982. Under Communist rule, the November anniversary of the Russian Revolution of 1917 has traditionally been marked by massive parades that show off the Soviet Union's military power. Above, rows of tanks rumble majestically through Moscow's Red Square while (opposite) a huge portrait of the revolutionary leader V. I. Lenin surveys the scene.

Then, boarding his jet, Gorbachev headed south for Malta and his next appointment, on the storm-tossed waters of Marsaxlokk Bay, located near the southern tip of Italy in the Mediterranean Sea.

The giver of freedom

The Czech students, religious people in the USSR, the people at the Berlin Wall hacking their one-time prison to pieces — all of these people had two things in common. First, all had suffered under the rule of Communism, with its demand for unquestioning obedience to an all-powerful state. Although they all had strongly desired change, they were powerless to bring it about. Second, all had been freed from oppression by Mikhail Gorbachev, the leader of the world's most powerful Communist country.

Thanks to him, the Soviet tanks did not come back to Prague. Thanks to him, the Berlin Wall would soon become a memory. Thanks to him, Ukrainian Catholics living in the Soviet republic called the Ukraine, who had been forced to worship in secret, could now openly proclaim their faith.

Mikhail Gorbachev's direct authority ended at the now tattered boundary between East Germany and the West. But his influence extended far beyond this border. It extended to millions of people all over the world who had lived in fear of the cold war and who worried that it could become "hot."

But the war the people feared was not a conventional war. This war would be a nuclear one, fought with weapons that threatened the destruction of all life on earth. Never before had a world leader taken such a strong, active stand against nuclear buildup. As Mikhail Gorbachev himself had said: "There would be neither winners nor losers in such a war. There would be no survivors. It is a mortal threat to all."

The Soviet Union was the country believed by the West to have been the biggest threat to peace in the world. Yet its leader, Mikhail Gorbachev, had made one of the most important moves toward resolving the conflict between the two sides since the cold war began. Thanks to him, this too is a nightmare for the whole world that is beginning to fade.

The man with iron teeth

Presidents Bush and Gorbachev were the two most powerful men in the world. But in the winter of 1989, there was no question whose power and influence showed more clearly.

With his friendly smile and his easygoing manner with the press and the public, Mikhail Gorbachev did not seem like most people's idea of a man who changes history. People who knew him, of course, also knew the courage, determination, and awesome intelligence that the genial exterior hid. They also knew the ruthlessness with which he pursued his goals. As another Soviet statesman once said: "This man has a nice smile, but he has iron teeth."

The phrase "iron teeth" hardly seemed to fit with the image of the liberator, the man who lifted fear from millions. But anger and fierce determination was another of the gifts that Mikhail Gorbachev put at the service of the ideal that dominated his life. His ultimate aim was to end the nightmares in the Soviet Union and to stop them from ever returning.

Turning obstacles into tools

By 1990, Gorbachev was well on the way to accomplishing his goals. In the Soviet Union, things that once seemed impossible were now everyday occurrences. There was the promise of religious freedom, the opening of borders to the West, and the new tolerance of opposing viewpoints.

Certainly, obstacles still faced him that would demand all the courage and dedication he could bring

Safe — in a dangerous world. Flanked by his grandparents, Misha Gorbachev stares warily at the camera in a Privol'noye backyard. Later, Misha's grandfather encouraged his education and lent him books from his well-stocked library.

to them. But obstacles did not daunt him, for he had proved throughout his career that overcoming them was his strength. The real secret of Mikhail Gorbachev's power was that he could always, when least expected, turn obstacles into tools. Then he could use them to make the impossible come true.

Misha's dangerous world

This man, who was able to achieve the impossible, was born in a time and a place where even survival was a matter of luck. Mikhail Sergeyevich Gorbachev, the son of a Russian peasant, was one of the lucky ones who survived a deadly famine.

"Misha," as he was called by his family, was born on March 2, 1931, in his parents' two-room hut in the village of Privol'noye. Privol'noye is in the far south of the Russian Soviet Federated Socialist Republic, in the Stavropol region between the Black Sea and the Caspian Sea. Even now it is an undeveloped place. Ducks and geese are often seen parading down the village's only paved street past the villagers' one-story homes. At the time of Misha's birth, the village was even more primitive.

A Russian village in those days was a dangerous place to be — especially for children. In nearby villages, all the children between one and two years of age would die before the end of 1933. They would not be the only ones to die. All through the USSR's "breadbasket," the great farming area that stretched from the Ukraine down into the Russian republic, many people who grew grain would be dying of starvation.

Stalin's plan

When Vladimir Ilyich Lenin, leader of the Communist party, took command in the Russian Revolution of 1917, Joseph Stalin was one of his lieutenants. After Lenin died, Stalin took control of the huge "new" country and ran it ruthlessly. He created an apparatus of terror that used spies and execution squads. He also expanded the prison-camp system called the Gulag.

The USSR, Stalin believed, needed two things above all else. First, the country needed more heavy industry — more coal, more steel, more factories.

Joseph Stalin was born Iosif Dzhugashvili. He took the name Stalin — "man of steel" — when he became active in revolutionary politics.

Above: The death of a policeman, as the Russian Revolution of 1917 burst into sudden life. The ruling caste of Russia had repressed the ordinary people for centuries. In 1917, the people seized power for themselves.

ОРУЖИЕМ МЫ ДОБИЛИ ВРАГА
ТРУДОМ МЫ ДОБУДЕМ ХЛЕБ
ВСЕ ЗА РАБОТУ, ТОВАРИЩИ!

Right: Working hard over an anvil, a man and a woman illustrate the Communist ideals of courage, comradeship, and work in a poster published in 1920. The new government improved the lives of ordinary working people. Special schools were set up to teach the country's millions of illiterate children and adults to read and write.

Before the revolution of 1917, the country had been far behind the industrialized European countries and the United States. After the revolution, the new Communist government was involved in a long and bitter civil war against supporters of the repressive tsarist regime. This regime had been ruthlessly ruling Russia for hundreds of years. The Soviet government was also busy fighting off attacks by Western countries that were hoping to take advantage of the new government's shaky and disorganized condition. In the course of this war, much of the industry and rail system of the country was destroyed.

The other thing that Stalin felt was needed was more food. In order to increase industrial production, more people would be needed to work in the factories. The number of people in the cities, where the industry would be developed, would increase. There would be a greater need for food in these areas. To grow more food, Stalin turned the land itself into a factory.

The peasants' small plots were taken away from them. So were their tools and animals. The land was divided up into big farms called "collectives," and the peasants were forced to work on these farms. The collectives sold part of what they grew to the government, at prices determined by the state. As part of their pay, the peasants got a share in whatever was left over.

Many peasants hated the collectives. They refused to work on them. Some killed their animals rather than give them to the state. The biggest threat to the plan came from the wealthier, landowning peasants. These people were referred to as *kulaks*. They opposed the plan more than anyone else because they had the most wealth and property to lose.

So Stalin decided to deal harshly with those who wouldn't cooperate. Thousands upon thousands of peasants and small farmers were sent to prison and many were executed. The exact numbers are not known, but it is estimated that millions of people died as a result of the conflict over collective farming.

Paying with their lives

Meanwhile, in the towns and cities, Stalin's plan for industrializing the country was working. By 1931, the year Misha was born, Soviet industry was growing as

World War II comes to the Soviet Union. In this photograph, taken in 1941, women in the Crimea search through the bodies of victims of Nazi killer squads for the bodies of their loved ones. The Soviet Union suffered terribly in both world wars. During the second, twenty million Soviets died.

never before. But there was a heavy price to be paid for this growth. And it was the peasants who paid it.

The workers who powered the industrial boom all had to be fed. To feed them, the government took more and more of what the collective farms grew, leaving the farm workers less and less. In Misha's area, the year before his birth, the government had taken almost half the harvest. In 1931, it took almost two-thirds. The peasants' share of the food they grew got smaller and smaller each year. The death toll of the peasants quickly rose into the millions.

But by March 2, 1933, Misha Gorbachev had passed his second birthday and survived.

War comes to South Russia

Misha was an only child, but not a lonely one. In a place like Privol'noye, everyone knew everyone else, so he was not short of friends. Like other village children, he went to primary school when he was eight years old. The year was 1939. That year saw the outbreak of World War II.

War came to South Russia in 1941. That year Germany invaded the Soviet Union. All the young men in the area, including Misha's father, Sergei, were drafted. Bombs started to fall and, in Stavropol, the invading Nazis rounded up the Jewish people in the city and shot them in the main square. For days, eyewitnesses would recall, the sidewalks and roads would be stained with their blood.

Many people packed up all of their possessions and moved to places where life was less dangerous. But the Gorbachevs didn't leave. Meanwhile, away on the Polish front where he had been sent to fight, Sergei Gorbachev escaped from the fighting with only a minor wound. He returned to his home and resumed his previous career as a tractor mechanic and farm machine operator.

Heat, dust, and challenges

Usually, Soviets who lived in rural areas started work when they were sixteen. But so many Soviets were now being killed or wounded that the Communist party leaders decided that children should work too. From the middle of the war on, all children over twelve had to complete fifty working days a year, tending the crops or harvesting them.

Misha Gorbachev started his farm service in 1945, the year peace returned. He was fourteen. Every summer, he joined his father and another family in the fields, perched high on a combine, a machine that harvests grain. The heat, the dust, and the twelve-hour days were all daunting, but the young teenager accepted them as a challenge.

In 1949, a bumper harvest year, the Gorbachev team won a special award from the Soviet government for its work. Sergei and his son became holders of the Red Banner of Labor.

After the harvest was in, Misha made his first move away from the village where he was born. He went to high school in Krasnogvardeyskoye, ten miles (16 km) away from Privol'noye. Here he got high grades in almost all the subjects he studied.

Under the huge Russian sky, farm workers of the 1940s get the precious harvest in. When Misha Gorbachev first started helping his father in the fields, war and drought had brought Soviet harvests down to famine level. But by 1949, local harvest yields had improved enough to bring the Gorbachevs a state award for productivity.

He was good at other things as well. Some of his old schoolmates can still remember him acting in school plays, dressed as a Russian prince and dominating the stage. Others saw him as a leader — the sort of person that people listened to. He certainly was listened to by members of the school's Young Communist League, or Komsomol. Most young Soviets belong to this youth movement. Misha helped run the school branch.

"The sort who felt he was right"

With his family background, it would have been unusual if he hadn't joined the Komsomol. Like other people his age, he could remember Stalin's brutal farm program. But Gorbachev, like most others, never thought of questioning the system that had produced such horrors. The party was the party. It was the background to all life in the Soviet Union. And Stalin was its leader. For a Russian teenager of the 1940s, it would have been almost impossible even to imagine a different way of running the Soviet Union.

With problems he could grasp, however, Misha Gorbachev was not afraid of speaking out. His high

Moscow State University, where, in the 1950s, Mikhail Gorbachev first made contact with big-city life and with foreigners. It was also the place where he met his wife.

20

school girlfriend, Yulia Karagodina, remembers how he would argue with his teachers. He was not afraid to criticize them openly. Once he confronted a history teacher who he felt was extremely incompetent. "Do you," he once thundered, in front of his surprised classmates, "want to keep your teaching certificate?"

Protected by his self-confidence, he survived this battle and went on to fight others — with teachers, with Komsomol members. Even Yulia, who produced the school Komsomol newspaper, was not above criticism. Once, when she fell behind with her deadlines, he scolded her sharply in front of all the other members of the staff.

"He was the sort," Yulia would recall many years afterward, "who felt he was right and could prove it to anyone."

Moscow State University

In 1950, Mikhail Gorbachev took two steps that were vitally important to his future. Like his grandfather and father before him, he applied for membership in the Communist party. He also enrolled at Moscow State University. This was considered to be the best university in the Soviet Union.

Getting in was difficult, but his fine record and the Red Banner of Labor award must have helped. His party membership application must have helped his chances of being accepted, too. Less than a tenth of all Soviet citizens belonged to the Communist party of the Soviet Union. It was considered to be a special honor. So Communist party membership marked a person as someone special.

The subject Gorbachev studied at Moscow State University was law. The decision to study law seems like an unusual choice for someone who came from a rural farming community. He survived the tough five-year program and emerged at its completion with a law degree. He also fell in love.

The woman he had fallen in love with was named Raisa Maximovna. Her home was far away in the eastern part of the Soviet Union, in a region called Siberia. She'd come to Moscow to study philosophy. Gorbachev met her at a ballroom dancing school. Gorbachev had gone there to make fun of his friends

"Working people were justly indignant at the behavior of people who, enjoying trust and responsibility, abused power, suppressed criticism, made fortunes and, in some cases, even became accomplices in — if not organizers of — criminal acts."
Mikhail Gorbachev, describing the Soviet Union under Leonid Brezhnev in Gorbachev's book Perestroika

who were taking dancing lessons. But he came away dazzled by the beautiful Raisa, with her high cheekbones and her brilliant smile.

The orator's trade

Raisa and the law degree were not the only things that Moscow State University brought the young man from Privol'noye. It also turned him into an outstanding public speaker. Good courtroom lawyers have to be effective speechmakers; in the Soviet Union, as in the West, lawyers are carefully taught all the tricks of the orator's trade.

As his classroom arguments show, Gorbachev was naturally gifted at expressing himself in public. Later, as the leader of the Soviet Union, he would become one of the most important communicators the Soviet leadership had ever known.

Another of Moscow's gifts was just as important in a very different way. The city brought him his first contacts with the sophisticated world of the West.

At school and in the city of Moscow itself, Gorbachev encountered students from all over the Soviet Union. Many of them had served in World War II. Through discussions and arguments with these students, Gorbachev learned about life outside his own narrow field of experience. His roommate for the five years he attended the university was a Czech student named Zdenek Mlynar.

Intelligent, self-confident, energetic, and a good public speaker, Gorbachev as a student already had many of the marks of a successful politician.

The influence of the West

There was probably a price tag on this arrangement. Soviet students who had a lot of contact with foreigners were often asked by the security police to spy on their friends. So foreign students were sometimes surrounded by an invisible network of watchers, ready to report on the actions of the foreign students to the government officials.

The two law students got along very well together, even though their family backgrounds were very different. Gorbachev was from a small farming community. Mlynar's home was a modern, industrial country that, until World War II, had been part of the Western economic community.

Gorbachev absorbed a lot from his Czech roommate about things like clothes and style. In return, he gave his friend something infinitely more precious — his trust.

The official version of Soviet history, like everything else dictated by the Communist party, was at that time beyond question. The Gulag waited for anyone who dared disagree with it openly. But Misha Gorbachev once confessed to Mlynar that he had found a place in the official versions of Lenin's life where he felt the books contained information that was not true.

Mlynar never forgot the conversation. Not many Soviet citizens would have confided such doubts to a foreigner. For a person in Gorbachev's position, a labor award holder, a party member, a zealous officer in the university Komsomol, the confession was extremely unusual and risky.

Changing careers

After graduating from the university, Mikhail Gorbachev went back to his homeland in South Russia and settled in the town of Stavropol. He immediately faced a problem. He came to the realization that he didn't want to work as a lawyer.

At that time, the state's legal departments were overloaded. Stalin had died two years before, and very slowly, his system of terror was beginning to be taken apart by the new leaders of the government. People who had been imprisoned in the Gulag could now be given their freedom — as long as lawyers could get through all the necessary paperwork.

Gorbachev, like all new graduates, knew he would be assigned to his first job by the state. He also knew what it would be. He would help to clear up the huge rehabilitation backlog. This meant dealing with the complicated process of releasing prisoners and placing them back in society.

He looked around for a way out and found one. The state would allow him to refuse the job he was assigned to under one condition. He would have to work directly for the Communist party. He would have to become a party official.

Gorbachev got a job in the Stavropol Komsomol. The job itself wasn't especially good. But the decision

23

to apply for it was important. The young law graduate had found a new career in Soviet politics.

The way up the ladder

While Raisa worked as a teacher, her husband settled into his Komsomol job. He visited local branches, organized meetings, and spoke at youth conferences. He also made friends and contacts with helpful people that would be very important to him as he climbed the career ladder.

Being sociable and energetic, Gorbachev had no trouble fitting in. He impressed his first boss, who soon promoted him. He was promoted again, this time to the top local Komsomol job. Another problem now faced the ambitous young Gorbachev. Now in his early thirties, he knew he couldn't go on doing youth work forever. So once more, he changed from one career ladder to another. Rather than continue working in the Communist youth organization, he got a new job as an agricultural official.

This move was a gamble that nearly didn't pay off. Gorbachev had spent his childhood on farms working with tractors. But even with this experience, he didn't know enough about the complicated business side of farming to do his new job properly. He realized that he needed training. He needed more education. Without delay, he began a correspondence course in agricultural economics.

Getting his degree took him five years. By the time he got it, he was moving up the career ladder through the ranks of local party officials. His degree in agricultural economics helped push him farther and faster. In 1970, when he was thirty-nine, he got the top party job in the whole area. As far as Stavropol was concerned, he had reached the top of the ladder.

The big break

Right away, though, he found a new set of ladders in front of him. As Stavropol party boss, he now had access to the most powerful people in the Soviet Union — the party leadership in Moscow.

In 1971, his contact with the most powerful party leaders got closer, for he became a member of the

Central Committee of the Communist party. In 1974, he also became Stavropol's representative in the Soviet parliament, called the Supreme Soviet. Four years later, he got the biggest break of his career. The party was looking for someone to run the agricultural program of the whole country.

Swathed in plastic to keep the rain off, a Soviet consumer examines vegetables in a market stall to see if they're worth the price.

The party leaders agonized over their choice because they felt that each of the suggested candidates were unqualified in one way or another.

In the end, they settled on someone who was not the obvious choice at all. They picked Mikhail Gorbachev, the man they had met when they visited Stavropol to take vacations. The Stavropol region had become popular because of its mineral pools, clean air, and pleasant climate.

If Gorbachev was not anyone's preferred candidate, at least he wasn't anyone's enemy. He was

25

pleasant, he was hard-working, and he obviously did his job well. And the established leaders felt that this newcomer wouldn't be likely to throw his weight around or make things awkward for them. He seemed like the right person for the job.

In December 1978, Gorbachev moved with Raisa to Moscow to begin his new job. At the age of forty-seven, he had arrived at the heart of Soviet politics.

The government and the party

As important as the Supreme Soviet was, the party's Central Committee was an even more powerful group. The Soviet Union operated a "watchdog" system of government. One group, the Communist party, watched over the government, which carried out policies and enforced laws. The government itself, referred to as the Supreme Soviet, with its president and its ministers, actually ran the country, while the party, in effect, told them how to run it.

The Communist party made decisions about how the government bodies, like the agricultural department, for example, should perform their functions. Mikhail Gorbachev, the party boss for agriculture, had become one of the most powerful men in the country.

The following year, he moved even closer to the innermost circle of power. He became a junior member of the Central Committee's most powerful group, the Politburo.

The Politburo (short for "Political Bureau") is where the party's really big decisions are made. These decisions affect every part of life in the Soviet Union. The person who presides over the Politburo is the most powerful person in the whole country. As general secretary of the party, the leader of the Politburo is considered to be one of the two most powerful people in the world, equaled only by the president of the United States.

In 1978, the general secretary of the party was a man named Leonid Brezhnev.

"The greatest difficulty in our restructuring effort lies in our thinking."
Mikhail Gorbachev,
in Perestroika

The state's business

Brezhnev, the party, and the national government shared the responsibilities of governing the country. As the head not only of the government but of all business as well, they ran things much more directly than a government does in the West. They did not merely control national services like defense. They also controlled the way the people of the Soviet Union worked and conducted business.

From agriculture to cars, there was scarcely anything in the country that was not the government's business. The government, in fact, *was* business.

First it decided what food, raw materials, and equipment the country needed. Then it decided how the needs should be met. Decisions were made as to how much food should be grown, how much coal should be mined, and how much machinery should be made. It also decided what prices should be charged for everything that was grown or produced. The prices of essential things, like bread or gas, were kept very low so that everyone could afford them. Other things, like

Washing clothes through a hole in the ice. The lives of Soviet women have always been hard. Modern technology made housekeeping easier, but Soviet-made household gadgets often broke down. In Brezhnev's USSR, efficient tanks had a higher priority than efficient washing machines.

Opposite: As spring comes to the countryside, villagers pick their way past muddy snowdrifts left over from the long Soviet winter. The harsh climate is partially to blame for many of the problems of Soviet life, like food shortages. Floods resulting from a spring thaw can devastate crops just as badly as a summer drought.

televisions and heating for houses, were even supplied free. A huge army of officials, or bureaucrats, had the job of ensuring that all of these decisions about production and prices were carried out.

A system like the Soviet one, in which the state is the main planner, producer, and employer, is called a centrally planned economy. The government decided to produce so many million tons of grain, so many million tons of meat, so many billion kilowatts of electricity, so many tractors, refrigerators, tanks, etc. On paper, the plans containing these targets look reasonable. Everything is organized. Production will grow as planned, and people's lives will become better, richer, happier. It is as neat as a shopping list.

But it did not work in the Soviet Union.

The long wait

Below: In the Soviet Union, everyone spends hours standing in lines to buy scarce goods.

For most of the people of the Soviet Union, life was a constant struggle. It was not the heroic struggle of the revolutionary period, nor was it the nightmare of Stalin's time. It was just the day-in, day-out grind of

waiting in lines to buy food and other necessary goods which were often in short supply.

On average, people spent as many as fourteen hours a week standing in long lines. In the government-run shops, they waited for things like soap, children's toys, or sausage. They waited for boots for their family to wear through the fierce Soviet winter. If something really scarce came on the market, like carpets, they'd often stand in line for a whole day. Sometimes after waiting in line, the shoppers would find out that the stores had run out of the products that were in such great demand.

Shortages and shoddy goods

From carpets to ball-point pens, there were always shortages. Things came on sale and then vanished again. Somewhere along the way, a bureaucrat had made the wrong decision about ordering goods or distributing them. Or a factory manager hadn't met the target. Or between factory and shop, goods had just been misplaced or stolen. Possibly they had been siphoned off to the "black market." This was the unofficial, illegal system of buying and selling goods outside of the government-run stores. In the black market, many products could be purchased that were not available in the official stores.

The black marketeers did very good business. So did another set of traders, the farmers who grew vegetables or raised animals on their private plots. They were allowed to sell these without going through the state system. If people were desperate for fresh tomatoes or fresh meat, the farmers' market was sometimes their only way of getting them.

Naturally, the farmers charged as much as they could get. But even though the price was high, the quality was high too. As all Soviet shoppers knew, the quality of the goods in the state shops could hardly be worse. The refrigerators did not chill, the milk was thin, and the winter boots fell apart in the snow.

The new aristocrats

For ordinary people, then, life in the Soviet Union could be bleak and depressing. If you ran out of

The men at the top. Leonid Brezhnev, former leader of the USSR, is shown here with other party leaders at a parade in Red Square in Moscow.

something, you would have no idea when you'd be able to replace it.

The Soviet Union was meant to be a classless society. That means that no person in the society should have any more wealth or privileges than anyone else. The originators of this concept of society felt that it was unfair that some people should be extremely rich while others did not have enough to eat or a decent place to live.

But after Stalin took power, a new upper class was created in the Soviet Union. It was made up of the political leaders of the country.

And by Brezhnev's time, these new aristocrats and their families enjoyed many privileges that ordinary citizens did not have. They could walk into a special food store, fill a shopping bag with sausage and fresh fruit, pay a few rubles, and walk out. In Moscow, this was called "the Kremlin ration."

It was the same with medicine. Medical services were free, but the supply of drugs, like everything else, was erratic. For an ordinary person, even aspirin could be hard to get.

As is the case in the United States, the quality of Soviet health care varied greatly according to a person's wealth and status in society. When powerful party leaders became sick, they'd be taken to the special "Kremlin hospital," where the doctors used the latest equipment and the best, most efficient drugs. This was not the case with the average Soviet citizen. Like many people in the United States, they had to wait longer and received lower-quality health care than the people with more power and money.

The land without hope

For the people of Brezhnev's era, there was very little hope of changing the system or moving to a different country. They had to get the government's permission even to move from their homes to Moscow — or anywhere else in the country.

There was only one power center and one political organization in the Soviet Union — the Communist party. Doing anything that called the party and its policies into question was a crime. And the whole

"There is virtually no unemployment. . . . Health care is free, and so is education. People are protected from the vicissitudes of life, and we are proud of this. But we also see that dishonest people try to exploit these advantages of socialism; they know only their rights, but they do not want to know their duties: they work poorly, shirk and drink hard."

Mikhail Gorbachev, on the Brezhnev legacy, in Perestroika

31

apparatus of prisons and work camps still awaited those who committed such crimes.

Crimes and punishments

For dissidents with a lot of political influence, there were other subtle ways of enforcing silence. Until the 1970s, the world-renowned Soviet cellist Mstislav Rostropovich and his wife, Galina, belonged to the Soviet elite. Then Mstislav Rostropovich did something the government thought unforgivable. He came to the defense of writer Aleksandr Solzhenitsyn.

Nobel Prize winner Solzhenitsyn, famous for his *Gulag Archipelago*, a powerful and very detailed account of the Soviet work camps, was already under attack from the Soviet system. Soon, he would be deported. Meanwhile, the authorities punished his friend Mstislav by keeping him from continuing his musical career. His concerts were canceled without

Even for the genuinely ill, conditions in this modern Soviet psychiatric hospital seem to fall well below Western standards. Using "medical treatment" to punish dissidents, some Soviet psychiatrists aided the government in its repression and punishment of political prisoners.

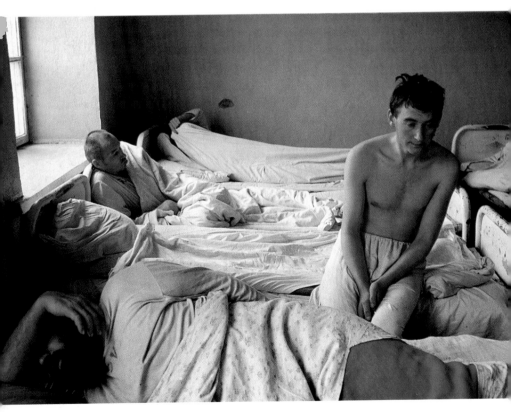

32

warning. Radio listeners no longer heard his work. The same thing happened to Galina, who had been a star of the Bolshoi Opera.

In the end, they managed to leave the country. But huge numbers of people were not able to move to a place that was more tolerant of their beliefs. It is estimated that by the early 1980s, the work camps still contained about two million people.

But there was another place of punishment that was feared even more. Some of the government's most outspoken critics were sent not to the Gulag but to psychiatric hospitals where doctors declared them to be criminally insane. In these hospitals, the political prisoners were often treated very harshly, and they usually had little hope of being released.

Shortages, police spies, and the work camps were some of the worst aspects of Soviet life as the 1970s turned into the 1980s. There was a great deal of unhappiness and dissatisfaction among the Soviet

Imprisoned for his beliefs. A photograph taken in 1971 captures the despair of "psychiatric patient" Yuri Titov, a KGB agent who became a Christian. At the end of the Brezhnev era, about a thousand dissidents were being held in psychiatric hospitals like the one shown here.

people during this period. This was the troubled country that Mikhail Gorbachev, the new agriculture boss, was to help rule.

The harvests that failed

Within the top ranks of the party, the position of secretary of agriculture (Gorbachev's new title) had a record of failure. Few people survived it with their reputations intact. There was so much that could go wrong in the huge country, and it all went wrong so often. Right away, it went wrong for Gorbachev too.

In 1978, the winter came early and gripped hard. In 1979, the sun parched the grain fields, and the harvest was bad. To feed its people, the Soviet Union imported grain from other countries. The harvest of 1980 was also bad. In vain, Gorbachev struggled to overhaul the farming system. But the harvest of 1981 was catastrophic, and that of 1982 was not much better.

Someone would certainly be held accountable for the low output of grain, which was not high enough to meet the country's needs. And it was obvious who it would be — Mikhail Gorbachev. He was by now a full member of the Politburo. His position was saved only by a stroke of luck. The meeting at which he would have had to deliver the bad news about the harvest was fixed for mid-November. A few days before this scheduled meeting, seventy-six-year-old Brezhnev died. The party needed to find a new leader.

In the political turmoil that followed, no one bothered about things like demoting the agriculture boss. Besides, Brezhnev's successor was a reformer who had become friendly with Gorbachev while vacationing in Stavropol. Gorbachev, then the local party leader, would welcome the high-ranking officials to the region, in accordance with party protocol.

Wanted: someone younger

Brezhnev's successor was another aging man — Yuri Andropov, who was sixty-eight and was the head of the Soviet secret police. They were called the Komitet Gosudarstvennoy Bezopasnosti (KGB), which means "Committee for State Security." Within a few months, Andropov became ill. But he tried to set his own mark on the system he ruled.

What he planned for the struggling Soviet system was a revolution. He intended to clean up the party. He wanted to curb the leaders' privileges. He also wanted to replace incompetent officials with ones who really knew their jobs.

As his illness grew worse, Andropov realized he needed someone who could stand in for him when he was too ill to attend meetings or make speeches. He needed someone who was competent, hard-working, decent, and honest. Andropov needed to look no further than his secretary of agriculture, Mikhail Gorbachev, for his second-in-command.

The travels of "Mr. G"

Soon Gorbachev was one of the most important men in the country. He had also begun to be known in the

Boris Pasternak was the author of the world-famous novel Doctor Zhivago. *He was unpopular with the Soviet authorities, and they did not allow his book to be published. So he smuggled it to Italy for publication there. When, in 1958, it won the Nobel Prize, the government forced him to refuse the prize. But when he died in 1960, Soviets crowded to his funeral (opposite). Today, his grave is a place of pilgrimage.*

West. In 1983, he led a group of top Soviet politicians to Canada.

The Western media, used to the serious and reserved officials that the USSR sent overseas, got a surprise. Here was a top party official who was actually friendly and outgoing. He enjoyed meeting people. He enjoyed discussions, even if they were challenging. If challenged, he fought back hard.

In 1984, Gorbachev visited Britain, and the British were just as surprised as the Canadians had been. This man from the Kremlin was more than just open and approachable. He was actually friendly! Everyone liked him and respected his views, even if they didn't agree with him. The British press nicknamed him "Mr. G." The British prime minister, Margaret Thatcher, praised him as someone she "could do business" with. This was a very unusual reaction to someone who was the leader of a country thought to be the most feared enemy of the Western nations and their way of life.

Above: When Mikhail Gorbachev came to power, official portraits always showed him without the birthmark on his forehead.

Old leader, new leader

By this time, Andropov had died. His job as general secretary of the party had been taken by someone who was even older. Konstantin Chernenko was seventy-two and already sick when he took the job. He was so ill that he could barely make a speech at Andropov's funeral. It was not hard to see what the future held for the Soviet leadership. Nor was it hard to see who might one day control it.

On March 13, 1985, after just one year in office, it was Chernenko's turn to be carried to his grave near the Kremlin's walls. And standing right behind the coffin was the new general secretary of the Communist party — Mikhail Sergeyevich Gorbachev.

A vast nation

The country that Gorbachev took over from Chernenko is the largest in the world. It counts its people in hundreds of millions and its size in time zones — eleven in all, from the Pacific Ocean to the Baltic Sea.

Opposite: "Mr. G" greets well-wishers in London. His habit of plunging into crowds to shake hands delights Westerners as much as it horrifies his bodyguards.

As vast as it is, its influence in 1985 stretched over an area that was even larger. All down its western frontier, protecting it from the West, lay a row of

Communist buffer states. These countries, referred to as the Eastern bloc, included East Germany, Poland, Czechoslovakia, Hungary, Romania, and Bulgaria. All of them were run by the local Communists according to the party doctrines of the Soviet Union. All had the Soviet mix of central planning, shortages, and fear.

Beyond the row of buffer states lay the West, and the nations that the Soviet Union feared so much. These Western nations feared the Soviet Union just as much. Not long before, U.S. president Ronald Reagan had called the Soviet Union the "evil empire."

Both sides had been locked for many years in a spiral of arms production, making weapons ranging from handguns to nuclear missiles. Each worried that the other one would build more destructive weapons. With better weapons, one side would be able to attack the other and defeat it in a war. That side would then be the most powerful in the world.

For the Soviet Union, as well as the United States, military might was, and is, one of the most important planning goals. Their best brains, their best equipment, and gigantic sums of money are used to develop weapon systems. In 1984, one-eighth of the USSR's total income went to weapon factories.

Gorbachev with his young daughter, Irina. Soviet people are discreet about the private lives of their leaders, and the "real" Mikhail Gorbachev is still a man of mystery. Very little is known about his tastes, his hobbies, and his family.

Feeling his way

Mikhail Gorbachev inherited an extremely troubled nation. Would he be able to cure its ills?

Curing the USSR was a great challenge. At first, Gorbachev took his time attacking the problems. He cracked down on the growing problem of alcoholism, especially as it related to reducing people's output and efficiency at work. He urged industry to be more efficient. And he helped boost the supply of food by encouraging Russians to lease little state-owned plots of land and develop them on their own.

He also visited factories and hospitals. He talked to workers and listened carefully to their complaints. A phenomenally hard worker, he set an example to other party officials. He arrived at the Kremlin early and stayed far into the night. And although he used a big limousine for his travels, he did not sweep down his route to the office in a grand procession. The general secretary's car went without an escort.

But things like alcoholism were only part of the problem. While he began to tackle them in these ways, Gorbachev was also pondering the best way to get at the core of the problem. Very quickly, he figured out how he would do it.

Perestroika

Gorbachev summed up the solution in a single word — perestroika, which means "restructuring" in Russian. Another way of describing what he had in mind would be giving the Soviet system "a good shakeup."

It was clear that the country had lost its way. And the trouble seemed to lie deep inside the way the Soviet economy worked.

In capitalist countries, the person who produced something tried to please the consumers who bought it. If consumers weren't pleased, they took their business elsewhere and bought another producer's goods. The producer either went out of business or modified the product to satisfy the demand of the consumers.

But that couldn't happen in the Soviet Union, where private firms were illegal and business was run by the government. If Soviet consumers didn't like what the government produced, they had no choice. They either bought it or did without whatever that product was. There was no competition among producers. This meant that producing higher-quality or more attractive goods was not rewarded.

The courage to be honest

Gorbachev's plan for reform was to tighten the reins on the Soviet Union. He was very blunt about what he wanted to change about the system. Basically, he expected everyone to work "an extra bit harder" — as hard as he worked himself.

"I like this phrase," he comments in the book he wrote explaining his great plan. "For me it is not just a slogan, but a habitual state of mind. Any job one takes on must be grasped and felt with one's soul, mind and heart; only then will one work an extra bit harder."

Perestroika, Gorbachev explained, meant expecting more of everyone in the Soviet Union. It meant making industry more efficient; it meant paying attention to what ordinary people wanted.

"The worker or the enterprise that had expended the greatest amount of labor, material and money was considered the best."
Mikhail Gorbachev, describing the Soviet Union under Leonid Brezhnev in Perestroika

"These changes are to be welcomed, because they are linked to the will of the people . . . to give a more democratic human face to those societies and to open up to the rest of the world."
Mikhail Gorbachev, speaking about revolutions in Eastern Europe

Meeting people. Gorbachev's greatest asset is his gift for communication. He can talk; he can also listen — and understand what the person is really trying to say. He is in his element in crowds (above); he's also at home drinking tea in someone's living room (opposite, bottom). The top picture on the opposite page shows him talking to staff members at the devastated nuclear reactor at Chernobyl.

It also meant having courage — the courage to seek change, the courage to face criticism, and the courage to be honest.

Among the challenges that Mikhail Gorbachev took on, honesty was the biggest challenge of all. For many decades, the Soviet government had not been honest with its people. Nor had it allowed them to voice their own feelings openly and honestly. It had attempted to smother all criticism, silence protesters, and enforce its rule of silence with fear.

Gorbachev said that the government's lies and deceit had to stop. The leaders needed to know what the people thought of them. The reason was a simple one and, in his book, he explains it very clearly. "We want more openness about public affairs in every

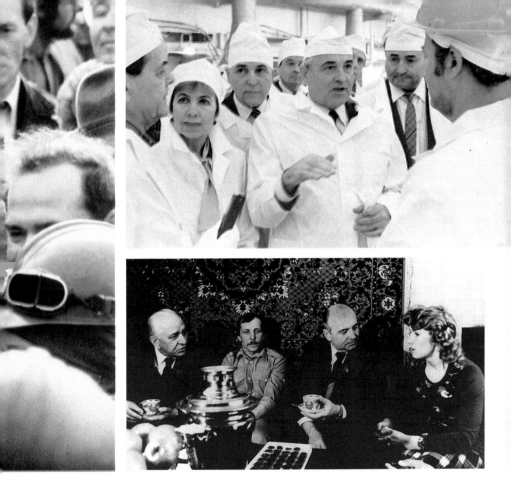

sphere of life. People should know what is good, and what is bad, too, in order to multiply the good and to combat the bad."

The Russian word for "openness" also meant "publicity." It was *glasnost*. All over the world, *glasnost* would soon become a word of Russian that everyone knew.

Openness and restructuring were the remedies that Gorbachev was proposing for his sick, secretive country. He was proposing nothing less than a second Russian revolution.

Chernobyl

As 1986 got under way, so did Gorbachev's great plan. Beginnings are often hard, and the start of

"An individual must know and feel that his contribution is needed, that his dignity is not being infringed upon, that he is being treated with trust and respect. When an individual sees all this, he is capable of accomplishing much."

Mikhail Gorbachev,
in Perestroika

41

On April 26, 1986, the nuclear reactor at Chernobyl in the Ukraine caught fire. Radioactive material pouring out of the damaged reactor (opposite) spread westward across Europe as far as Britain, and over 100 thousand people living in the area had to leave their homes (below). For the first time, Gorbachev's policy of glasnost allowed open discussion and reporting.

glasnost was no exception. That year, his country became the scene of the world's worst nuclear accident. On April 26, the nuclear reactor at Chernobyl, a city in the western region of the Soviet Union, caught fire and a great radioactive cloud spread over the whole area near the plant.

At first, the leaders of the USSR did not release information about the accident. But after two days, they allowed the story to break. After a week, it became clear just how big the disaster had been. On May 14, Gorbachev found himself announcing that 9 people had been killed, 299 injured, and 92 thousand evacuated from the area.

This was openness — with a vengeance.

The pace speeds up

Little by little, the pace of glasnost sped up. In August, a newspaper in the little Baltic republic of Estonia ran a story that would have been unprintable only a few

years earlier. Soviet soldiers, it said, had protested when the government extended their tour of duty at the stricken Chernobyl facility. The soldiers were afraid of the harmful effects of exposure to radiation. The story continued, stating that they had actually gone on strike! This type of action was unheard of in the Soviet Union.

Although part of the Soviet Union, Estonia, for a short while, had been an independent country. But in 1940, the USSR had taken it over, along with nearby Latvia and Lithuania. All three countries remembered their lost freedom with bitterness. So it was not surprising that the Estonian press was so quick to take the creator of glasnost at his word. Quickly, the challenge spread eastward. By late summer, journalists in other areas of the Soviet Union were demanding the freedom to speak their minds legally.

In December, the Soviet rulers freed one of their most distinguished and outspoken critics. This was nuclear physicist Andrei Sakharov, the Nobel Prize winner whose battle for human rights had condemned him to internal exile seven years earlier.

In January 1987, the KGB dismissed a top officer. He had invented criminal charges against someone who had threatened the Communist way of doing things. Making false charges had been standard Soviet practice for years. But this time, the KGB officer had attempted to falsely accuse a reporter working on a story about abuses of power.

A month later, the government freed 150 of the Soviet Union's political prisoners. This was the first trickle of what would soon become a flood.

In August, the Baltic states became even more daring about expressing their anti-Soviet feelings. People protested in the streets against their resented overlord. Amazingly, the authorities let them do it.

In 1988, all children in Soviet schools heard that their final history exams had been canceled for that year. The textbooks they had used were being re-written. The new books would tell the truth about Stalin and the USSR's past.

Thaw

And so it continued — a gradual easing of pressure, a thaw in the ice. Something else was thawing at the

43

same time — the cold war. If Gorbachev wanted to cure the USSR of its sickness, its costly weapons mania was one of the main symptoms he had to treat.

If the Soviet Union scaled down its military might, more money and expertise would become available for other purposes. Raising the Soviet standard of living, for instance, was high on the list. It would be much easier if the United States agreed to scale down its own military power, too. But, for the Americans to do that, they had to believe that the Soviets weren't trying to trick them into a position of weakness.

After many years of hostility and harsh dialogue between the two world powers, this would not be an easy task. Leaders in the United States had to see Gorbachev as someone who could be trusted. Once again Gorbachev was able to achieve what many people thought was impossible. By the end of 1987, he had gained the trust of the U.S. government.

By then, Gorbachev had already met then president Ronald Reagan twice to talk about arms. The first meeting was held in Geneva, Switzerland, in the winter of 1985. As far as specific agreements or treaties, the meeting did not achieve much. But it was crucially important in another way. Meeting face to face at what became known as the "fireside summit," the two most powerful men in the world found they got along well

May Day. The first day of May is an important holiday in the Soviet Union, and May Day parades are another occasion for the Soviets to show off their military power. Here, photographed in the 1960s, rows of nuclear missiles are wheeled into Red Square.

with each other. Of course, they needed interpreters to communicate. But even in translation, they found they "spoke the same language."

The "mighty tree"

A second summit followed, in the Icelandic capital of Reykjavik. And in December 1987, the leader of the Soviet Union met with President Reagan in the United States. In front of television cameras that beamed the event all the way back to the USSR, Reagan and Gorbachev signed a treaty. This treaty was an agreement to reduce the size of both countries' enormous nuclear missile stockpiles.

"We can be proud," Gorbachev commented, "of planting this sapling, which may one day grow into a mighty tree of peace." President Reagan ventured into Russian himself, reciting his much-quoted phrase. It was *Doveryai no preverya*: "Trust — but check."

"You repeat that at every meeting," quipped the Soviet leader, as the people who had gathered there burst into laughter and applause.

They've got to go

Gorbachev's great plan was moving ahead. But it was still moving rather slowly, especially at home in the

45

Soviet Union. There were people who believed that Gorbachev should be doing much more to reform the country. And there were many who said he should be doing much less!

Perestroika and glasnost were not good news for the privileged party leaders set in their comfortable ways. These leaders, as well as the Soviet citizens who preferred to keep things the way they were, began to voice a growing opposition to Gorbachev's plans for restructuring the Soviet system. Some people felt that he was destroying the achievements of the society in his attempt to rid it of its evils.

Gorbachev might have been the most powerful man in the Soviet Union. But he was still not safe from challenge by enemies within the party. To protect his position and keep his program of reform alive, he began to oust his critics from their high-level jobs.

Planting a "tree of peace" for the world. In Washington, Mikhail Gorbachev and President Ronald Reagan sign the huge document containing their agreement to reduce the number of nuclear missiles.

Then, in 1988, he decided to enlist another ally — the people of the Soviet Union. Direct contact with the ordinary party members was not a common occurrence for a high-ranking Soviet leader.

In June 1988, he called a special meeting, an "extraordinary party congress." This was the first such meeting to have been held since 1941. From all over the Soviet Union, five thousand party delegates gathered in Moscow at the Palace of Congresses. And there, on June 28, they heard their leader attack the enemies of his plan.

Gorbachev's message was clear and direct. The enemies of his new program of reform had to be removed. "We have no right," said the party general secretary, "to permit perestroika to founder on the rocks of dogmatism and conservatism, on prejudices and personal ambitions."

And he concluded the historic meeting by outlining a new plan for keeping his experiment afloat.

Free elections!

"We are learning democracy and glasnost," Gorbachev explained, "learning to argue and conduct a debate, to tell one another the truth." Democracy meant involving ordinary working people in government. It meant slimming down one inefficient government body, the Supreme Soviet, and giving more power to another one, the Congress of People's Deputies. And it meant free elections.

Free elections! It was unheard of. The elections that everyone was used to were quite different. When Supreme Soviet members were elected, everyone turned out to vote. But in each area, they had only one person to vote for. This was the person the party had chosen. It was all *pokazuka*, or a show. It was the old Soviet way of doing things, the very opposite of glasnost.

The five thousand delegates to the party conference took these amazing proposals rather calmly. They applauded in the right places, but that was all. But there was nothing calm about the reaction of the Soviet people when, on March 26, 1989, they turned out to vote for the people they wanted.

Over half the voting areas offered a choice of two candidates. Some offered three or more. It was no

"The nations of the world resemble today a pack of mountaineers tied together by a climbing rope. They can either climb on together to the mountain peak or fall together into an abyss."

Mikhail Gorbachev,
in Perestroika

surprise that most of the deputies chosen were party members. But the voters had some big surprises in store for the party itself. In Leningrad, for instance, they gave a flat "no" to the city's party boss and to his second-in-command. They also rejected the city's mayor and *his* second-in-command. Nor was that the only place where voters expressed dissatisfaction and a desire for change.

At last, the monopoly of the party aristocrats was beginning to crumble.

"Perestroika itself can only come through democracy."
Mikhail Gorbachev,
in Perestroika

The year the world took fire

The Soviet Union had its first free elections. This alone would have made 1989 a year for the world to remember. But there would be more.

After 1989, little in Gorbachev's empire would ever be the same again. It was to be a year of revolutions, the year that, for the countries of Eastern Europe, the world took fire. And it was Mikhail Gorbachev himself who put the match to the tinder.

The blaze started in East Germany, the Communist state that had been created when Germany was divided after World War II. Along its border ran the "iron curtain." This was a virtually impenetrable barrier of barbed wire and watchtowers that marked the westernmost edge of the Communist bloc. The iron curtain also surrounded the western part of Germany's traditional capital, Berlin.

West Berlin was a unique place. It was a little part of West Germany that had been marooned far away in the East, behind the iron curtain. For its frontier, it had the notorious Berlin Wall, built by the Communists in 1961. Until then, huge numbers of East Germans had escaped through Berlin to the other, richer half of the divided country. The wall, guarded by armed soldiers, made escape nearly impossible.

The people of the German Democratic Republic (East Germany) never forgot the country to the west. Over there, people seemed to have better jobs, homes, lives. There were no work-place spies and no secret police. The system of fear stopped at the border. West Germany seemed like a better place to be.

In the summer of 1989, these pent-up hopes and fears boiled over, and the people who felt imprisoned

Opposite: A woman casts her vote in the first free elections to be held in the Soviet Union. Several top Communist leaders lost their positions.

49

by their system found a way out. The easiest way out was through Hungary's border, for in that country, Communist power was itself fading. Thousands of escapees made the journey, then tens of thousands.

"Gorby! Gorby!"

Meanwhile, people who wanted to live a happier life in East Germany had also begun to make their views known. They were taking to the streets in protest. One of their chants was "We want to stay!" Another named the only man who might help them: "Gorby, Gorby!"

It was at this point that, on October 6, Mikhail Gorbachev himself flew to Berlin. The aim of his visit was to celebrate East Germany's fortieth birthday. But it was no birthday present that Gorbachev, who had by then been appointed the USSR's president (leader of the nonparty section of government), brought the East German authorities. It was the very opposite.

A nightmare come true

As the country seethed in protest, the Soviet leader addressed its rulers at Berlin's Palace of the Republic. They blanched as he told them that Moscow would no longer help to keep them in power. Naturally, he put his message in diplomatic code. "Matters affecting the GDR," he said, "are decided not in Moscow but in Berlin." But the East Germans got the point.

They got it even more plainly the next day, when Gorbachev met the East German leader, Erich Honecker. This time, the Soviet president was extremely blunt. He told Honecker that rulers who did not respond to their people's wishes "put themselves in danger."

He went on to be blunter still. "Those who delay," he said, "are punished by life itself."

So there it was. The unbelievable was happening, not just within the Soviet Union, but in its empire as well. The Soviets no longer had their finger on the trigger, ready to crush protest wherever it appeared. No Soviet troops would come to Honecker's aid — not this time, nor ever again.

Honecker and the rulers of the other Eastern bloc countries were on their own now. For all of them, their worst nightmares had come true.

Taking to the streets

Gorbachev's jet was still in German airspace when the smoldering revolution below suddenly flared into life. Thousands of East Berliners headed to the Palace of the Republic, chanting and singing. To their old chant of "Gorby!" they added a new one: "No violence!"

With their usual brutality, the police attacked them, crushed the protest, and took five hundred protesters away to jail. But the protests continued to increase in size. By the end of October, hundreds of thousands of East Germans were taking to the streets in large protests and demonstrations.

Like Gorbachev himself, the protesters wanted glasnost and free elections. They also wanted the freedom to travel back and forth between their homes and the West. And they wanted to remove the hated Berlin Wall.

At first, East Germany's rulers put up a fight. As the demonstrations grew bigger, Honecker called in the East German troops and told them to fire on the

The East German leader, Erich Honecker, bends an ear to his guest during official ceremonies to mark the country's birthday. In just over a month, the prison doors would spring open. In fact, Gorbachev had hinted several months earlier that this might happen. When he visited West Germany in June, journalists asked him about the Berlin Wall's future. Nothing, he told them, was "eternal."

protesters. In Leipzig, where the main demonstrations took place, the people tensed themselves for dreadful bloodshed. But on Monday, October 9, fifty thousand of them defied the rule of terror.

They gathered in the dark outside the church of Saint Nicholas, where protest meetings were held every week. They marched through the streets to the great square named after communism's founder, Karl Marx. From there, the protesters paraded on around the city, along the road to the station. And once more, the unbelievable happened.

The troops watched them pass. Their guns stayed slung on their shoulders. Some even talked and joked with the marchers.

The Berlin Wall opens

Just in time, the protesters had been saved by colleagues in Honecker's government. With Gorbachev's words ringing in their ears, they had canceled the order to fire at the protesters. Two days later, they ousted Honecker himself. Then, faced with a country in tumult, they hurriedly started to introduce reforms.

On November 9, the Berlin Wall opened.

Dazed with delight, East Berliners flooded through the once deadly barrier. No border guards shot at them now. Instead, the soldiers in the brown uniforms joked with the crowds that streamed past. Meanwhile, in Moscow, the leaders of the Soviet Union expressed approval of the events taking place in East Germany.

The domino effect

The opening of the wall was dramatic enough. But it was only a beginning. Looking back on the situation, people would call it the start of a "domino effect."

The domino effect is what happens when dominoes are lined up in a row and the first one is knocked over. With smooth precision, the whole row topples over. The same thing happened that winter among the Communist governments of Soviet-controlled Eastern Europe. One after another, the unpopular governments toppled over.

After East Germany, it was Bulgaria's turn. On November 10, the Bulgarians forced the resignation of President Todor Zhivkov, the longest-serving ruler of

an Eastern bloc country. At seventy-eight, he had been in power for thirty-five years. Czechoslovakia, where Soviet tanks had helped crush the Prague Spring of 1968, was next.

Hungary and Poland scarcely counted in the dominoes' rippling collapse because they had fallen long before. In June the Polish people had voted out the Communists and voted in the newly legalized Solidarity party. Moscow, in the meantime, had stood by without taking any action. The Hungarians had agreed to do away with one-party rule back in January. Then, too, Moscow had let them do it.

The courage of desperation

The tiny country of Albania, ruled by old-style, hard-line Communists, remained isolated from the domino effect. As winter approached, it seemed as if Romania would not be touched by it either. Ruled by the brutal leader Nicolae Ceausescu, it was a country where fear of the government was widespread. But in mid-December, the Romanian people also joined Eastern Europe's great revolt.

53

With the courage of desperation, they turned on their rulers, defied their guns, and removed them from power. On Christmas Day, Ceausescu and his wife were executed by firing squad in a barracks courtyard.

An empire no longer

By the first days of 1990, Eastern Europe had changed completely. The one-time colonies of the Soviet Union were colonies no more. They had thrown out their Communist rulers. Through it all, the Kremlin had just stood by and watched these dramatic changes take place.

The people of Eastern Europe had won their freedom. But they could not have done it without the consent of Mikhail Gorbachev. He had radically changed the face of Soviet government.

Chicken — and progress

As the 1990s got under way, a Soviet housewife appeared on a Western television station and spoke her mind to the surprised audience. The interview took place in a food store. "There's no meat," the shopper said, gesturing to the shelves around her. "That's why I bought chicken."

With an ironic smile, she added: "That's progress!" And her statement showed that there was another kind of progress as well. Public statements criticizing the government or complaints about the system were no longer forbidden. This was a great contrast to Gorbachev's careful questioning of the system to his roommate in law school.

Then, in the early 1950s, Misha Gorbachev had dared to talk of his doubts only to a trusted friend. But now, almost forty years later, a Moscow shopper could grumble to a whole nation of foreigners seated before their television sets. And with her shopping bags, she could still walk home a free woman.

What glasnost has achieved

Outside the Soviet Union, Mikhail Gorbachev had transformed the Northern Hemisphere. The old fears and the old boundaries were being swept aside, and a new world was emerging.

Opposite: In Prague, Saint Wenceslas on his iron horse surveys the huge crowds that gathered daily in Wenceslas Square as Czechoslovakia's "peaceful revolution" gathered pace. When this photograph was taken, half a million people had packed themselves into it.

The longing for freedom also affected parts of the USSR itself. The republics of Lithuania, Latvia, and Estonia were among the leaders of this other struggle for independence. Above, in protest against Soviet domination, the people of the three Baltic republics form an unbroken human chain stretching 350 miles (560 km) through the three states. Right: Another republic, another protest. In the deeply religious Ukraine, Catholics proclaim their faith.

At home, changes had been slower to come. His reforms had not changed things in the way that mattered most to the ordinary citizens. That is, he had not yet adequately increased the availability of goods in the stores. As in Brezhnev's time, there was still no meat. The Moscow homemaker's ironic expression

Two sorts of weapons. In Bucharest (above), they used guns; in Prague (left), they brandished roses. The Czechs' nonviolence actually helped them to win their revolution, since it brought unshakable public support. But public opinion and the news media also played a key part in the much bloodier revolt in Romania, where much of the fighting focused on Bucharest's television headquarters. Even the trial of Romanian president Nicolae Ceausescu and his wife was shown on television. After their execution, so were their dead bodies.

In the Soviet republic of Turkmenistan, an old man prays in his local mosque. By 1990, the Muslims in the USSR's southern republics were also beginning to seek independence from the Soviet Union.

seemed to imply that having chicken in the store did not solve the whole problem of shortages either. Meanwhile, down in Gorbachev's southern Russian homeland, soap was now so scarce that people were rationed one bar every three months.

So the USSR was still struggling with perestroika. But glasnost was a different story. It was glasnost that, in the Baltic states, produced the banners saying "Red Army go home." It was glasnost that freed the dissidents and let them demand further, faster reforms. It was glasnost that allowed a Russian comedian to do a humorous impersonation of Gorbachev to a full house at Moscow's Variety Theater.

The four gifts of Mikhail Gorbachev

The freedom to break away, the freedom to speak one's mind, the freedom to make changes — these are three of the four great gifts that Mikhail Gorbachev brought the Soviet people. A politician of genius, he may bring more. He may also give them the prosperity they so desperately need. To achieve this, though, he and everyone else in the Soviet Union will have to work "an extra bit harder."

The fourth gift is not a freedom, but something even bigger. For the first time in Russia's long history, a Russian ruler has respected his people's right to full self-respect — the right to be themselves, to make their own decisions, to live their lives in dignity and peace. Once experienced, this right is not given up lightly.

Whatever happens in the future, the process cannot now be turned back. Liberty is now part of the Soviet Union's history.

For More Information . . .

Organizations

The following organizations can provide information about the Soviet Union, the Eastern bloc independence movement, Communism, and Mikhail Gorbachev. Write to them if you would like to know more about issues of interest to you. In your letter be sure to tell them exactly what you would like to know, and include your name, address, and age.

Forum for U.S.-Soviet Dialogue
c/o Paul Stephen
School of Law
University of Virginia
Charlottesville, VA 22901

Friends Peace Exchange
Box 390
Sandy Spring, MD 20860

The Information Department
    of the Soviet Embassy
1706 18th Street NW
Washington, DC 20009

Institute for Soviet-American Relations
1608 New Hampshire Avenue NW
Washington, DC 20009

People to People International
501 East Armour Boulevard
Kansas City, MO 64109

Perhaps . . . Kids Meeting Kids
    Can Make a Difference
380 Riverside Drive
New York, NY 10025

Books and Articles

These books and articles will give you more information about the events taking place in the Soviet Union today, as well as important events in Soviet history.

Lenin: Founder of the Soviet Union. Abraham Resnick (Childrens Press)
Mikhail Gorbachev: A Leader for Soviet Change. Walter Oleksy (Childrens Press)
Passport to the Soviet Union. Stephen Keeler (Franklin Watts)
The Picture Life of Mikhail Gorbachev. Janet Caulkins (Franklin Watts)
Portrait of the Soviet Union. Fitzroy Maclean (Henry Holt and Company)
"Soviet Disunion," *Time.* March 12, 1990.
The Soviet Union: The World's Largest Country. John Gillies (Dillon Press)
The Soviet Union. James Riordan (Silver Burdett)
"Starting Over: Gorbachev turns his back on Lenin," *Time.* February 19, 1990.
"A United Germany: The New Superpower," *Newsweek.* February 26, 1990.

Glossary

atheist
Someone who does not believe in the existence of a God or gods.

Baltic republics
The small Soviet republics in the northeastern section of the Soviet Union. They include Estonia, Latvia, and Lithuania. These countries were independent between the two world wars, but Joseph Stalin made them part of the USSR in 1940.

Berlin Wall
The barrier built by the East German government in 1961 to prevent people in East Germany from escaping to West Berlin. The wall was torn down in November 1989.

black market
A system of illegal trade that involves the selling of goods that are not available in stores. In the Soviet Union, products that are in short supply, as well as those that are not allowed by law, are often sold through the black market.

Brezhnev Doctrine
A policy established by Leonid Brezhnev in 1968. It stated that the Soviet Union had a right and duty to intervene whenever any country in the Eastern bloc turned away from Communism. It remained in force until Gorbachev rejected it in 1989.

bureaucrat
A government official who insists that all rules and regulations be strictly observed. This term is also used to refer to inefficient or corrupt officials who needlessly complicate and slow down the functions of government.

Central Committee
The key policy-making body within the Soviet Communist party. Within the Central Committee is a smaller group of powerful party leaders, called the Politburo.

cold war
The period of tension and suspicion following World War II when governments built up their supplies of weapons. The two most important participants were the Soviet Union and the United States. Mikhail Gorbachev and George Bush officially declared the cold war to be over in December 1989.

communism
A political system based on the idea that people as a whole rather than individuals should own the wealth, property, business, and manufacturing of a country. Ideally, communism's goal is to distribute wealth evenly and provide for everyone's needs.

Communist party of the Soviet Union
Also called *CPSU* or *the party*. This is the only political party allowed in the Soviet Union and the only body in the country that makes laws. There has recently been discussion of allowing opposition parties to compete for important positions in the government, but no rival parties have yet been formed.

democracy
A system of government which, in theory, is guided by the will of all citizens on an equal basis. This is accomplished through electing representatives who are supposed to act according to the desires of the people who voted for them.

dissident
Someone who doesn't agree with official policy. In the USSR, dissidents have campaigned for a more democratic and humanitarian system of government.

Eastern bloc
The nations of Eastern Europe dominated militarily, politically, and economically by the Soviet Union from the 1940s to the late 1980s. The bloc includes Poland, East Germany, Czechoslovakia, Hungary, Romania, and Bulgaria.

German Democratic Republic (East Germany)
Germany was split into four zones at the end of World War II. The British, French, and American zones were merged in 1949 into the Federal Republic of Germany, or West Germany. The Soviet zone became the separate nation of East Germany. It was a Communist-ruled country until 1989.

glasnost
The Russian word for "openness" or freedom of speech. Glasnost is one of Gorbachev's most important reforms, the right of individuals to say what they wish without fear of punishment. Under glasnost, Soviet citizens can criticize their government for the first time and offer suggestions for change.

Gulag
A Russian word that stands for the Chief Administration of Corrective Labor Camps. The Gulag was a system of prisons for dissidents and opponents of the government. Here they were forced to work long hours under poor conditions, causing the death of many from disease and starvation.

iron curtain
The name given by Winston Churchill to the border between Soviet-dominated Eastern Europe and the democracies of the West. Originally an imaginary barrier, in the 1950s it became a real one when East Germany erected barbed-wire fences to prevent people from crossing the border into West Germany.

KGB
The Komitet Gosudarstvennoy Bezopasnosti (Committee for State Security). The Soviet secret police, an agency which is responsible both for controlling anti-Soviet activity within the USSR and for coordinating Soviet spying and intelligence operations in other countries.

Komsomol
The Soviet Union's Communist youth movement, also called the Young Communist League. Membership is required for anyone who wants to join the Communist party. Gorbachev's first official post was as an officer of the Komsomol.

Kremlin
The ancient walled city in the heart of Moscow which serves as the seat of the Soviet government. The name is often used to stand for the government itself. For example, "the Kremlin announced its new policy on nuclear testing today."

Lenin, Vladimir Ilyich (1870-1924)
Born Vladimir Ulyanov, Lenin was the revolutionary leader who masterminded the Communist victory in the Russian Revolution of 1917. As the first leader of the

USSR, he defeated the anti-Communist forces and their French, British, and American allies in the civil war of 1919-22. He is honored by Communists everywhere as the first Communist head of state anywhere in the world. His tomb in Moscow, where his body is on display in a glass coffin, is a national shrine.

perestroika
The Russian word for "restructuring." This is the name given to Gorbachev's plan to make the Soviet government and economy more efficient.

Politburo
A shortened name for the Political Bureau of the Central Committee of the Communist party. The Politburo makes all the most important decisions regarding government policy. The general secretary of the party chairs the Politburo.

republic
In Soviet terms, the individual states that make up the Soviet Union. Some of them were separate nations, such as Lithuania and Latvia. Others are regions within what was, before the Russian Revolution, the Russian Empire.

Russia
The former name of the country that is the largest of the republics that make up the Soviet Union. Many people still call the Soviet Union by this name.

Solidarity
A independent labor union organized by Lech Walesa in Soviet-controlled Poland in 1980. It was banned by the Polish Communist government the following year. The ban was lifted in April 1989 and Solidarity candidates ran against Communist opponents in June, winning landslide victories in the first two-party elections in decades. In September, a Solidarity prime minister took office, setting up the first non-Communist government in Eastern Europe in nearly forty-five years.

Soviet Union (*See* USSR.)

Stalin, Joseph (1879-1953)
The Communist leader (born Iosif Vissarionovich Dzhugashvili) who in 1924 succeeded Vladimir Lenin as the political leader of the Soviet Union. He ruled the country as an absolute dictator from the late 1920s until his death in 1953. While Stalin is credited with transforming the USSR into a major industrial nation and world superpower, he was also responsible for ordering the deaths of millions of people. Among his many victims were the *kulaks*, or independent farmers, who opposed his nationalization of farming. He also exiled or executed anyone suspected of being his political enemy.

summit
A meeting of heads of governments or other high-ranking government officials.

superpower
A nation with strong economic resources and great military capability. Superpowers

exert pressure and influence on other countries because of their military and economic strength.

Supreme Soviet
Until Gorbachev's reforms, this was the USSR's parliament or law-making body. Its members had to be approved by the Communist party officials in their local areas.

USSR
The Union of Soviet Socialist Republics, often called the Soviet Union or Russia. It is the largest nation in the world and one of the most powerful. It is made up of fifteen "republics," which are somewhat similar to the American states or Canadian provinces. Most of them represent different ethnic groups — Russian, Ukrainian, Armenian, Lithuanian, and so forth.

Chronology

1905   A revolution breaks out in St. Petersburg, Russia's capital. The tsar, Nicholas II, is forced to promise reforms. He later breaks all his promises.

1917   **March** — A revolution forces Tsar Nicholas II to step down. A Western-style democracy is set up, with Aleksandr Kerensky as premier.
November — A second revolution overthrows the Kerensky government and places the Communists in control, with Vladimir I. Lenin as their leader.

1918   **July** — The tsar and his family are executed by the Communist government.
November — World War I ends. The United States and Great Britain ignore Russia in the division of postwar Europe. The United States, Britain, France, Poland, and Japan invade Russia in an attempt to overthrow the Communist government.

1924   Lenin dies, warning the party to remove Joseph Stalin from power.

1928   Ousting all rivals, Stalin begins to take total control of the Soviet Union. He launches the first Five-Year Plan to modernize industry and agriculture.

1931   **March 2** — Mikhail Sergeyevich Gorbachev is born in Privol'noye, in the Stavropol region of the Russian Soviet Federated Socialist Republic.

1934   Stalin begins a shakeup of all levels of government, ordering the death or imprisonment of anyone not loyal to him personally.

1941   **June 22** — German dictator Adolf Hitler invades the Soviet Union. The USSR suffers heavy casualties and joins the Allies.

1942   **December** — The USSR's German invaders are turned back at Stalingrad, after having conquered a large part of the eastern USSR.

1944-45 The Soviet armies occupy Eastern Europe, driving out the German forces. Poland, Bulgaria, Romania, Yugoslavia, Albania, and Hungary, as well as parts of Germany, come under Soviet control.

1945 World War II ends. The cold war begins.

1948 **February** — Soviet-backed Communists seize control of Czechoslovakia.
May — West Berlin is isolated by Soviet troops.
June — Yugoslavia breaks from Soviet domination and adopts a neutral position in the cold war.

1949 For his work on the land, Gorbachev is given a state award, the Red Banner of Labor.

1950 Gorbachev becomes a candidate member of the Communist party. He goes to Moscow State University, the USSR's most prestigious university, to study law. While there, he meets Raisa Maximovna, whom he later marries.

1952 Gorbachev becomes a full member of the Communist party.

1953 **March** — Joseph Stalin dies. He is briefly succeeded as leader of the Soviet Union by Georgi Malenkov, who is followed by Nikita Khrushchev.

1955 After graduation from the university, Gorbachev returns to Stavropol with Raisa, where he becomes an official of the local Komsomol.
May — The Warsaw Pact, a mutual defense treaty between the USSR and the nations of Eastern Europe, is established.

1956 Mikhail and Raisa's daughter and only child, Irina, is born.
Khrushchev denounces Stalin's excesses as crimes and promises a return to the ideals of Lenin.
December — Soviet troops put down a revolution against the Communist government in Hungary.

1959 Communist Fidel Castro overthrows the dictator of Cuba, making Cuba the first Soviet ally in the Western Hemisphere.

1961 **August** — The East German government builds the Berlin Wall between East and West Berlin in an effort to stop people from escaping to the non-Communist West.

1962 Gorbachev starts work for the Communist party as an agricultural organizer.

1963 Gorbachev becomes head of the agricultural department of Stavropol.
The Nuclear Test Ban Treaty becomes the first of a series of agreements between the United States and the Soviet Union to limit the arms race.

1964 Khrushchev is replaced by Leonid Brezhnev as general secretary.

1968   **August** — Soviet troops invade Czechoslovakia to crush a reform movement there. Brezhnev announces the Brezhnev Doctrine, stating that the USSR will intervene militarily to prevent any non-Communist or anti-Soviet governments from coming to power in Eastern Europe.

1969   U.S. president Richard Nixon and his adviser Henry Kissinger begin a policy of friendliness and cooperation designed to ease U.S.-Soviet tensions and promote cooperation between the two nations.

1970   Gorbachev becomes the Communist party chief of the Stavropol region. He is also elected to the Supreme Soviet.

1971   Gorbachev becomes a member of the Central Committee of the Communist party. He begins a series of trips to represent the Soviet Union abroad.

1972   The United States and the USSR sign the Strategic Arms Limitation Treaty (SALT), limiting the number of nuclear missiles on each side.

1978   During an agricultural crisis, Gorbachev is appointed as head of the Central Committee's agricultural department.

1979   **November** — Gorbachev becomes a nonvoting candidate member of the Politburo.

1980   Ksenia, the Gorbachevs' granddaughter, is born.
January — U.S. president Jimmy Carter announces an embargo on grain exports to the Soviet Union to protest its invasion of Afghanistan.
Summer — The Moscow Olympics are boycotted by the United States and sixty-four other nations to protest Soviet intervention in Afghanistan.
October — Gorbachev is named a full member of the Politburo.

1982   **November** — Brezhnev dies, age seventy-five. He is succeeded by KGB chief Yuri Andropov. Gorbachev becomes Andropov's close ally.

1983   **March** — Andropov suffers massive kidney failure. He survives but is terminally ill. As Andropov's health fails, he increasingly uses Gorbachev as his representative and spokesman.

1984   **February** — Andropov dies, age sixty-nine, after only fifteen months in office. The Soviet leadership passes to Konstantin Chernenko. Gorbachev is recognized as the second most important figure in the party.
December 10 — Gorbachev delivers a speech in Moscow in favor of *glasnost*, or "openness."

1985   **March 10** — Chernenko, age seventy-three, dies. Gorbachev is named his successor the next day. He has just turned fifty-four.
November — Gorbachev and U.S. president Ronald Reagan meet in Geneva, Switzerland, to discuss arms control and U.S.-Soviet relations.

1986   **April 26** — The world's worst nuclear accident takes place in the Ukraine when a reactor catches fire at the Chernobyl nuclear power plant. The fallout spreads throughout the Northern Hemisphere. Three days later, the Soviet Union publicly admits the incident.
October — The second Reagan-Gorbachev summit takes place in Reykjavik, Iceland. Gorbachev suggests a complete ban on all nuclear weapons. Reagan rejects the proposal.
December — In keeping with glasnost, Dr. Andrei Sakharov, Nobel Prize-winning human rights activist, is released from a Soviet prison.

1987   Mikhail Gorbachev's book, *Perestroika*, is published. It outlines his plans to reform Soviet society.
December — At the third Reagan-Gorbachev meeting, the two leaders sign a treaty agreeing to eliminate some types of nuclear weapons.

1988   **June** — At a special party conference, Gorbachev outlines his plans to pursue perestroika and to make the Soviet government more democratic.
October — Gorbachev is made president of the Soviet Union.

1989   Communist governments throughout Eastern Europe fall.
January — The Hungarian parliament passes laws permitting the existence of more than one political party, thus bringing Communist domination to an end.
March — The Soviet Union elects members of its new parliamentary body, the Congress of People's Deputies. Many party bosses and bureaucrats are defeated in public elections.
June — In Poland, the newly legalized Solidarity opposition wins a landslide election victory over the ruling Communists.
September — Hungary formally agrees to pass East German refugees on to West Germany. In East Germany, demands for reform increase.
October 6-7 — Gorbachev visits East Berlin. He tells East Germany's leaders that the Soviet Union will not intervene to keep them in power.
November 9 — The East German government opens the Berlin Wall.
December 1 — Gorbachev meets with Pope John Paul II. He promises to lift all restrictions on freedom of worship throughout the USSR.
December 3 — Gorbachev meets U.S. president George Bush at a summit in Malta. They officially declare an end to the cold war. Gorbachev later praises the changes in Eastern Europe.
December 10 — Czechoslovakia adopts a non-Communist government.

1990   **February** — In Moscow, 300 thousand people attend a demonstration calling for faster reforms. Gorbachev announces that the Communist party will no longer be the only political party allowed in the Soviet Union, ending the single-party rule that has existed for over seventy years.
March 11 — Lithuania declares its independence from the Soviet Union. The next day, Gorbachev announces that the move is invalid.

Index